Ying's

Best
ONE-DISH
MEALS

Ying's

Best
ONE-DISH
MEALS

Quick & Healthy
Recipes for the
Entire Family

Ying Chang Compestine

SELLERS
PUBLISHING

Published by Sellers Publishing, Inc.

Text © 2011 Ying Chang Compenstine
Photo Credits: pp. 27, 28, 36, 41, 42, 48, 67, 68, 81, 86, 91, 102 © Beth Galton;
pp. 47, 59, 63, 96 © Getty Images; pp. 53, 71, 95 © Getty Images/Beth Galton;
p. 60 © iStock/travellinglight; p. 112 © iStock/Louis Hiemstra; p. 113 © iStock/Kelly Cline;
p. 114 © iStock/whitewish; p. 115 © iStock/Susan Fox; pp. 32, 106 © Jonathan Kantor Studio;
pp. 35, 77, 78, 85, 99, 109 © Kirsten Strecker/Big Leo; pp. 54, 72, 92, 105 © Lisa Cohen

Sellers Publishing, Inc.
161 John Roberts Road, South Portland, Maine 04106
Visit our Web site: www.sellerspublishing.com • E-mail: rsp@rsvp.com

ISBN: 13: 978-1-4162-0643-9

Library of Congress Control Number: 2011921884

Printed and bound in China

Dedication

To my dear son, Vinson, Ming Da, I will miss you so much
when you go to college!

Contents

Meals in a Pot

Meals in a Hurry

Introduction

If you ever find yourself standing in the kitchen, wondering what to do for dinner after a long, hard day of work, or after chauffeuring the kids to and from school, music lessons, baseball practice, and the dentist's office, you might just find that these quick and delicious one-dish meals are the best answer.

Many of us struggle to find a balance between a concern for our family's well-being and the alleged convenience of processed and fast foods. In today's fast-paced culture, some of us don't realize that healthy meals can be flavorful while also being easy to prepare.

I don't think anyone should be subjected to hours of slaving away in the kitchen washing, chopping, slicing, roasting, and grilling after a busy day, just to provide their family with a healthy, tasty meal. Nor do I think that people should be condemned to peeling open plastic trays of frozen food or buying unwholesome take-out dinners because of the frenzied pace of our modern lifestyles.

With a son who runs cross-country, a husband who enjoys an occasional 80-mile bike ride, and my own passion for competitive badminton, our family is busy, active, and always ready for the next meal. Like most people, I don't have hours to spend in the kitchen preparing food, yet everyone in my family wants delicious, healthy food — right away. So I depend on quick, flavorful, and nutritious one-dish meals that use fast cooking techniques and require minimal cleanup. To speed up the process, I enlist my family's help. While spending quality time together, we get to do some things we all love — cooking and eating.

The following recipes are among my family's favorites. They have passed the three strict requirements of my sous-chefs — quick, healthy, and delicious.

By utilizing fresh prewashed and precut produce, many of the recipes take less than 30 minutes to prepare. With the time spent driving and waiting for an order of unhealthy fast food or budget-busting take-out meal, you could put a healthier, more affordable homemade meal on the table. Each dish is a satisfying meal, combining good proteins with high-fiber, vitamin-rich carbohydrates and fresh vegetables packed with antioxidants and phytonutrients. Many of the dishes are also low in sodium, which helps control high blood pressure and promotes a healthy heart.

I hope the recipes that follow will not only simplify your cooking experience but also make it more enjoyable. Why not start today? Pick one of these simple and healthy dishes and invite your family into the kitchen to cook and eat!

How These Recipes Were Created

My passion for food began when I was a young girl in Wuhan, China. I liked to follow Nai Nai, my grandmother, around the kitchen, watching her slice meat, pan-fry noodles, and cut tofu. Her skillful knife transformed bamboo shoots into miniature trees; green onions into brushes; and white onions, carrots, and radishes into flowers of all sorts. Along with the beautiful presentation, my grandmother always served vegetables, grains, and lean protein in equilibrium. She would find a task for my small hands so that I could be involved: shelling soybeans, or rinsing the rice between my little fingers. Best of all, I would get to taste what Nai Nai cooked before anyone else, including my voracious older brothers!

Years later, I realized that all that time in the kitchen with Nai Nai not only gave me an edge in my sibling rivalry, it also stirred my enthusiasm for cooking.

In 1987, shortly after I arrived as a graduate student at the University of Colorado in Boulder, I found myself sitting at a long, rectangular table surrounded by my host family. This was my first experience at a restaurant in the United States.

We exchanged small talk, and since I knew very little about American food, and was still shy about speaking English, I asked them to order for me. When the food came, I was shocked. Big cuts of meat and enormous unpeeled potatoes covered everyone's plate. Back home, Nai Nai would have made a meal for the whole family from the meat on just one of those plates, and she would have diced the potato into proper bite-size pieces instead of serving it whole! Later I learned that they had taken me to a well-known steak house. I nibbled a bit and waited, hoping that more food would come: vegetables, rice, or noodles. To my disappointment, the only other things brought out were slices of chocolate cake.

This was the first time I'd ever eaten a meal without green vegetables or grains. As for that big slab of meat, even with all my effort, I could bring myself to eat only a very small portion. And I was still hungry at the end of the dinner. For the next two years that I lived with them, I started creating recipes by mixing and matching the Western ingredients on hand with the Eastern skills I learned in my grandmother's kitchen. (In spite of our culinary disparities, they became my second family, and I lived with them until I received my Master's degree.)

These days, I divide my professional life between writing and public appearances. I spend a significant portion of my time lecturing around the world about healthy living and eating.

After each trip, I return to my kitchen inspired, and enthusiastically recreate the best dishes I tasted during my travels. It often turns into a little international tasting that I hold for my family and friends. I've served them annatto rice from South America; a shrimp pizza from Rome; a pasta dish I picked up while in Greece; Wasabi Salmon with Miso-Sesame Sauce from Kobe, Japan; and Spicy Sesame Pad Thai that I ate at a street vendor's stand in Pattaya, Thailand. I would mix and match my discoveries, while finding ways to simplify the steps, and use fresh, organic, easy-to-find substitutes for the less common ingredients.

I have always believed that food not only satisfies hunger, but it also plays an important role in our connection to others and to our past. Often when I cook certain dishes, they remind me of the places I have traveled, the people who taught me how to prepare the food, and the family and friends with whom I have shared meals. The recipes in this book are the favorites from these international tastings. They are one-of-a-kind, because they are my creations and my variations on simple and healthy meals from around the world, using ingredients that are readily available in local markets. I hope you will gather many happy memories as you enjoy these dishes.

How to Use This Book

I often tell people that cooking is a creative process. Use the recipes as a guide and experiment. Substitute fresh vegetables or fruits that are in season and grains that you have on hand for those called for in the recipes, and choose the spices to adjust the taste to your liking. In these flexible recipes, I provide tips on how to swap in your family's preferred ingredients for the less popular ones.

All the recipes in this book are one-dish meals with vegetables, grains, and protein. You can always pick a few dishes from each chapter and cook a feast for your family and friends. Any leftovers will make a great lunch.

Meal Planning

Master a few dishes: Select a few of your favorite recipes from this book to become your go-to weeknight dinners. Once you have mastered them, explore and sample other dishes. Let other family members take part in choosing what to eat.

Schedule meals: Plan meals for two or three days. Cook larger portions, and utilize leftovers from one meal for use in the next. For example, stir-fry extra cooked grains and pasta with fresh vegetables or other ingredients, or use leftover meat or seafood in soups or salads.

Share the cooking: Who said cooking is a grown-up's job? Kids love to cook, and they take pride in eating food they helped prepare! Get them involved in planning meals, shopping, cooking, and cleaning. Plus, what's a better way to catch up with each other's day than in a delicious-smelling kitchen? Divide the meal into parts and give each member a set task. Give children a safety lesson in the kitchen, and assign them the tasks that are appropriate for their age. Younger children can wash vegetables, mix salads, and set the table, while older children and adults can help prepare ingredients, cook, or clean.

About Grains

To save time, prepare extra grains or pastas on weekends. This will speed up the week-day's meals. Store the prepared grains in a sealed container in the refrigerator, and they will stay fresh for up to three days. Certain grains can easily be replaced for others. Knowing which are best for stir-fry and which are best in soups or stews can guide your substitutions. For example, either couscous or rice works nicely for stir-frying. Rolled oats are great for thickening soups. Steel-cut oats are a good substitute for beans in stews. They also take much less time to cook than dry beans.

Grains play an important role in a healthy diet. Because quinoa, oats, and couscous are high in protein, they provide a simple and healthy way to boost the protein content in any meal. Black rice rivals blueberries in anthocyanin content, which has proven to have antioxidant and anti-inflammatory properties. Its lush dark purple color also lends a colorful note to stir-fry.

Always rinse grains (except couscous) in cold water. Bring water to a boil in a big pot, stir in the grain. Reduce heat to low and simmer. Cover and cook the grain in a pot until it becomes tender and most of the liquid has been absorbed. To shorten the cooking time for barley, brown and black rice, soak them for 30 minutes or overnight before cooking. When stir-frying, make sure your grains are cold so they won't stick to the wok.

For your convenience, I have included a brief guide to whole grains that provides best use, protein content, and nutrition information on page 17. You can cook many grains in a rice cooker, but if you don't have one, follow the cooking instructions above and use the cooking time on the chart as a general guide.

Grain Cooking Guide

1 cup of grain	best use	liquid	cooking time	yield	protein content per 1 cup serving	rich in
Barley	Salads	2 cups	30–40 minutes	3 cups	4–5 grams	Niacin and iron
Couscous	Salads, Stir-fry	1¾ cups	Remove from heat and let stand for 5 minutes or until the liquid has been absorbed	3 cups	6 grams	Riboflavin, niacin, vitamin B6, folate, thiamine, pantothenic acid
Quinoa	Salads	2 cups	15–20 minutes	3 cups	5 grams	Lysene, iron, calcium, zinc, potassium, magnesium, phosphorus, and copper.
Rice, Brown	Stir-fry	3 cups	45 minutes	3 cups	3–5 grams	B vitamins, essential fatty acids, tryptophan, magnesium, manganese, selenium
Rice, Black (or Forbidden)	Stir-fry	1¼ cups	25–30 minutes	2 cups	5 grams	Anthocyanins, B vitamins, manganese, selenium, magnesium
Oats, steel-cut	Stews	3½ cups	30 minutes	3½ cups	10 grams	Betaglucan, B vitamins, vitamin E, copper, iron, zinc, magnesium, phosphorous, calcium, thiamin
Oats, rolled	Soups	2 cups	10–15 minutes	2 cups	10 grams	Betaglucan, B vitamins, vitamin E, copper, iron, zinc, magnesium, phosphorous, calcium, thiamin

Cooking and Storing Pasta

Various types of pasta require different lengths of cooking time. Follow the package directions. To prevent pasta from sticking, use plenty of water and don't overcook it.

Rinse cooked pasta in cold water. After draining, store it in an airtight container. It will stay fresh in the refrigerator for 3–5 days. An easy way to reheat pasta is to rinse it under hot water for a few seconds, then drain. Serve it with warm sauce or stir-fry with other ingredients. I do not recommend freezing pasta. Freezing can cause pasta to lose its fresh taste, and not all pastas are suitable for freezing.

Plan Ahead

Planning ahead is about investing a little time now to save more in the future. For example, if you have a busy night coming up, use your grocery store's salad bar to get a head start on that night's cooking by buying just the shredded or chopped vegetables, meats, fish, and nuts you will need. It will save time and money while reducing waste.

- Vary meals to keep them interesting.
- Make meal planning a family event. Let family members help select the meals that they want to eat.
- Do a weekly check of your basic ingredients. Prepare a list before you leave for the store. The list reduces duplication and forgotten items that lead to second trips and waste.
- Be mindful of avoiding waste when shopping for fresh ingredients.
- Thaw frozen foods you plan to cook that evening quickly in a bowl of warm water right after you get home.
- If you need to boil water for pasta, start heating it up right after you get home.

Get Organized

Through years of balancing my busy career with my family life, I have found that having a well-organized and well-stocked kitchen saves time and diminishes the temptation to surrender to processed foods that are overloaded with calories, saturated fats, sugar, sodium, and white carbohydrates.

- Keep your kitchen clean between meals to save preparation time and help you feel more motivated to cook.

- Arrange your kitchen so you can find things quickly. Store staples close to where you will need them. I keep dry spices, cooking oils, and sauces that don't need refrigeration near my stove.

- Always store your cooking items in the same place, so you know where to find them.

- Read the recipe for general ingredients before starting. If you don't have something, substitute it with the same category of food, such as barley for quinoa in a salad, brown rice for black rice in stir-fry, and chicken for pork.

- Preheat the broiler or oven while you read the recipe.

- Cut down on cleanup by reusing measuring cups and spoons, and by measuring dry ingredients before liquids.

- Use a nonstick wok or skillet. They are easier to clean.

Stock Up

A well-stocked kitchen is a time-sensitive cook's best friend. It gives you more options for quick meals that everyone will enjoy. It is important to keep a variety of grains, oils, veggies, sauces, and proteins on hand. Feel free to substitute fresh with frozen vegetables. Protein sources such as meat, seafood, tofu, and eggs can often be interchanged. The goal is to eat a balanced meal of grains, vegetables, and protein.

FRESH INGREDIENTS

Deli-cooked beef, turkey, chicken breasts, and ham
Skinless, roasted chicken breasts
Salmon fillets
Smoked salmon fillets
Eggs
Tofu, firm or extra-firm
Shiitake and oyster mushrooms
Green onions
Garlic
Ginger
Onions
Fresh vegetables, in-season
Precut, prewashed vegetables
Fresh, whole wheat noodles (take less time to cook than dry)
Whole wheat bread

FROZEN INGREDIENTS

Your favorite mixed vegetables

Shrimp, peeled

Salmon fillets

Frozen yogurt, ice cream

OILS AND SAUCES

Now you can easily buy many high-quality sauces at the supermarket. Using a flavored sauce can save time by reducing the number of ingredients you have to prepare. For example, using garlic-seasoned vinegar and spicy sesame oil adds the flavors of garlic and chile to a dish without the peeling and chopping.

Chili garlic sauce

Soy sauce

Spicy stir-fry sauce

Seasoned vinegar (such as roasted garlic or chile pepper)

Seasoned pasta sauce (such as basil or garlic)

Toasted sesame oil

Curry paste

Smooth peanut butter or almond butter

Fish sauce

Extra-virgin olive oil

EQUIPMENT

The beauty of one-dish meals is that they require minimal equipment, and each meal calls for just a single skillet, pan, or pot — making cleanup a snap.

Knives: Good, sharp knives speed up the task and make cooking more enjoyable, as well as safer. A 6-inch knife for peeling and slicing and a 10-inch chef's knife for slicing and chopping should be sufficient for most of the recipes in this book.

Cutting boards: Wooden cutting boards are easier on knives. Use them when slicing meats and hard vegetables. Wash them with hot, soapy water and dry thoroughly right after use. Plastic boards are easier to clean and dishwasher-safe. Use them for small chopping chores and leafy vegetables.

Always cut fresh vegetables, fruits, and foods that do not need further cooking before cutting raw meats. Or use one designated cutting board for raw meat and seafood, and the other one for foods that do not need further cooking.

Rice cooker: A rice cooker is a good appliance to have for quick meals. Besides cooking rice, it can also cook other grains. You simply add the water to the grains, turn on the switch, and attend to your other tasks. The rice cooker will signal when the grains are cooked. High-end brands like Zojirushi Rice Cookers allow you to set the time when you want the grains to be cooked and ready. Many rice cookers come with grain/water measuring instructions.

Pans: A chef's pan is like a mini wok. It has deep, gently sloped sides. It is practical for sautéing, simmering, and boiling. Find one with a hard-anodized aluminum surface that won't chip, stain, or scratch. A 6-quart pan is a good choice for a family of four. The surface is dishwasher-safe.

Wok: A traditional iron wok is big and heavy, especially when it's loaded with food. A 12-inch wok should be sufficient for a family of four. Look for a one with a cover and handle that will remain cool to the touch while cooking. Find one with a hard-anodized aluminum surface that won't chip, stain, or scratch and is easy to clean.

Skillet: A skillet with a flat bottom and vertical sides is ideal for sautéing, searing, and low-heat cooking. A 12-inch skillet that comes with a lid should be sufficient for most purposes. Look for one that has a hard-anodized aluminum surface that is scratch-resistant and easy to clean.

Soup pots or stockpots: They are available in different sizes. A 6.5-quart stainless-steel pot or a 4-quart cast-iron pot can serve most of your needs. Some stainless-steel pots also come with steamer baskets, which are ideal for steaming vegetables and warming leftover foods.

Meals in a Wok

Perhaps I am biased, but I love stir-fry! It's what I ate for nearly every meal while growing up in China. The quick, energetic pace of stir-fry makes it a great match for the busy Western lifestyle, as individual fresh ingredients quickly meld to take on a new, delicious, healthy form. Stir-frying is easier than ever now that precut vegetables and sliced meats are readily available in supermarkets, along with flavored sauces and oils. If you do a lot of stir-frying, you may want to buy a wok, but a good skillet or chef's pan will also do the trick. Because of its fast pace, be sure to have all your ingredients ready to go. You wouldn't want to overcook your meal while looking for your seasonings. Once you master this skill, you will appreciate the timesaving aspects of this technique.

Candied Walnuts with Shrimp in Spicy Garlic Sauce

Walnut shrimp may be a popular dish at your favorite Chinese restaurant. However, if you are as health-conscious as I am, you may scamper away from the deep-fried, covered-in-starch battered shrimp. In this version, the shrimp is marinated in a simple, spicy sauce, and then sautéed with bell peppers and onions to establish an exciting flavor without the extra fat and mess of deep-frying. Make sure you have plenty of cooked rice or pasta to go with this fiery dish.

Serves 4

Spicy Garlic Marinade

3 large garlic cloves, minced

¼ teaspoon crushed red pepper (or to taste)

1 tablespoon olive oil

1 tablespoon fresh lemon juice

1 teaspoon salt

1 pound medium raw shrimp, shelled and deveined

3 tablespoons extra-virgin olive oil

2 medium bell peppers, any color, julienned

1 small white onion, halved lengthwise and thinly sliced

1 teaspoon salt

¼ teaspoon crushed red pepper (or to taste)

½ cup candied walnuts, to garnish

Combine marinade ingredients in a large bowl. Add shrimp and toss to coat. Cover and refrigerate for at least 30 minutes.

Heat a nonstick wok or sauté pan over high heat and coat with 2 tablespoons oil. Add shrimp, reserving marinade. Sauté until shrimp turns pink, about 2 minutes. Remove and place in a bowl.

Recoat wok with remaining 1 tablespoon oil. Add peppers, onion, salt, red pepper, and reserved shrimp marinade. Sauté until peppers soften, about 1 minute. Return shrimp to wok, stir, and heat through. Garnish with candied walnuts. Serve hot with rice or pasta.

Per serving: 364 calories; 26 g protein; 25 g fat; 10 g carb; 3 g fiber.

Happy Family Stir-fried Rice

During traditional Chinese holidays, families gather for a big feast. Near the end of the meal, everyone enjoys this dish, which symbolizes harmony and happiness. These themes are represented by the many ingredients that go into the dish; each ingredient complements the others to create a greater meal as a final result. Using precooked rice from the refrigerator not only saves time on busy weeknights, but the cold rice won't stick to the wok or pan.

Serves 6

3 eggs
¼ cup minced red onion
1 small fresh red chile, minced
2 teaspoons low-sodium soy sauce
3 tablespoons olive oil
3 cloves garlic, chopped
1½ cups fresh or frozen and thawed
  mixed vegetables
1 medium red bell pepper, seeded and
  chopped into 2-inch chunks
3 cups cooked rice
Salt and pepper to taste
2 teaspoons sesame oil
3 tablespoons toasted pine nuts or other
  nuts (optional), to garnish

In a bowl, beat eggs well. Mix in onion, chile, and soy sauce. Heat 2 tablespoons olive oil in a medium nonstick wok or skillet over medium-high heat. Swirl to coat. Add egg mixture. Swirl to evenly cover bottom of wok. Cook without stirring until eggs are firm and brown on the bottom, about 1 minute. Flip eggs and brown the other side. Chop eggs into small pieces with spatula. Remove eggs from wok and set aside.

Heat remaining 1 tablespoon olive oil in the same wok. Add garlic and stir-fry until fragrant, about 30 seconds. Add mixed vegetables. Cook and stir for 1 minute. Add bell pepper and cook and stir for another minute. Mix in rice. Cook and stir until rice is heated through. Return egg mixture to wok and mix well. Season with salt and pepper. Drizzle with sesame oil and garnish with toasted nuts. Serve hot.

Per serving: 293 calories; 8 g protein; 14 g fat; 35 g carb; 2 g fiber.

Kung Pao Pork with Soba Noodles

Kung Pao (pronounced Gung Po) originated in the Sichuan Province of central-western China. In this traditional dish, small slices of meat are marinated in a sauce and stir-fried with dry chile peppers and fresh vegetables, and then garnished with peanuts. If you are pressed for time, use frozen vegetables. This ginger-soy marinade is so simple and delicious; don't be surprised if you soon find ways to use it with your favorite chicken, firm tofu, or fish recipes. Soba noodles are made with buckwheat flour and are found in the Asian food section of most grocery stores. You can substitute thin spaghetti for the soba noodles.

Serves 4

Ginger-Soy Marinade
1 tablespoon minced fresh ginger
1 tablespoon bottled minced garlic
1 teaspoon cornstarch
2 teaspoons low-sodium soy sauce
1 teaspoon water
1 teaspoon sake (rice wine)

*1 (¾-pound) pork tenderloin,
  fat trimmed*
8 ounces soba (buckwheat) noodles
1 teaspoon plus 2 tablespoons olive oil
2 cups (¼-inch) sliced green bell pepper
1 (8-ounce) package shredded carrots
¼ cup water
*1½ tablespoons thinly sliced green
  onions*
2 tablespoons chili garlic sauce
1 tablespoon fresh lemon juice
*¼ cup chopped dry-roasted peanuts,
  to garnish*

To prepare marinade, combine all ingredients in a large bowl, and mix well. Cut pork into ½-inch-wide strips. Combine pork with marinade. Let stand for 5 minutes.

Prepare noodles according to package directions. Toss with 1 teaspoon olive oil. Transfer to a large serving dish and keep warm.

Heat remaining oil in a large nonstick skillet or wok over medium-high heat. Add pork mixture, and stir-fry for 3 minutes or until pork loses its pink color. Add sliced bell pepper and shredded carrots, and stir-fry for 1 minute. Stir in water, onions, chili garlic sauce, and lemon juice, and cook, stirring, for 2 more minutes.

Serve warm over noodles, garnish with peanuts.

Per serving: 470 calories; 24 g protein; 10 g fat; 72 g carb; 4 g fiber.

Longevity Noodles with Chicken

The peanut sauce in this dish also goes well with grilled chicken, and it makes an excellent dip for crisp, sliced vegetables. To save time during the busy week, make the sauce in advance on the weekend. Be sure to include lightly salted, crunchy sunflower seeds. They are packed with vitamins and important minerals. When paired with slightly sweet cranberries, they give this dish a fresh spin that will delight all ages. To save time, buy shredded vegetables at a salad bar.

Serves 6–8

Peanut Sauce
2 teaspoons olive oil
2 tablespoons minced onion
1 teaspoon grated fresh ginger
1 garlic clove, minced
½ cup soy milk
¼ cup creamy peanut butter
1 teaspoon fresh lemon juice

8 ounces cooked noodles (see cooking
   instructions on page 18)
8 ounces chicken breast from deli or
   flavored tofu, cut into thin strips
½ cup snow peas, trimmed, and shredded
½ cup packaged shredded carrots
¼ cup toasted, lightly salted sunflower
   seeds
2 tablespoons dry cranberries

To prepare sauce, heat oil in a small saucepan over medium-high heat. Add onion, ginger, and garlic, and sauté for 5 minutes or until onion is tender. Stir in soy milk, peanut butter, and lemon juice. Cook, stirring constantly, for 3 minutes or until peanut butter is completely melted. Remove from heat and let cool completely.

In a large bowl, combine noodles, chicken, snow peas, and carrots. Pour peanut sauce over and toss well. Sprinkle with sunflower seeds and dry cranberries before serving.

Per serving: 225 calories; 15 g protein; 11 g fat; 18 g carb; 2 g fiber.

Pan-fried Tofu Salad with Green Tea and Honey Dressing

To me, green tea and tofu seem to go hand in hand; green tea's delicate flavor beautifully complements tofu's mild taste. The backdrop of salad greens highlights the colors and textures of the pears and tomatoes. The green tea dressing will go well with any fresh salad.

Tofu, a complete protein, is rich in vitamins and minerals, including folate, potassium, and fiber, much like other soy foods, which when combined with the antioxidants in green tea provide an exceptionally healthy, nutritious dish.

Serves 4

Green Tea and Honey Dressing
½ cup boiling water
2 green tea bags
½ green onion, minced
2 tablespoons fresh lime juice
1 tablespoon honey
½ tablespoon fish sauce
2 cloves garlic, chopped

1 block (12.3-ounce) package extra-firm
 tofu, drained
2 tablespoons olive oil
2 teaspoons loose green tea leaves
1½ tablespoons sesame seeds
⅛ teaspoon salt
4 cups gourmet salad greens
2 cups cubed Asian pears or ripe pears
1 cup halved cherry tomatoes
 (about 8 ounces)

To prepare dressing, pour boiling water over tea bags in a medium bowl. Brew 3 minutes, then discard tea bags. Combine tea and remaining dressing ingredients. Set aside.

To prepare salad, place tofu on a flat surface and press out water. Dry with paper towel. Cut tofu into 8 equal squares. Heat olive oil in a large nonstick skillet or wok over medium-high heat. Add loose tea leaves, sesame seeds, and salt. Stir-fry for 30 seconds or until fragrant. Arrange tofu on tea leaves mixture in skillet, and pan-fry for 6 minutes or until golden brown, turning after 3 minutes. Place tofu slices on paper towel.

Combine greens, pears, and tomatoes in a salad bowl. Drizzle with dressing and toss well. Arrange 1¼ cups salad on each of 4 plates. Top each serving with 2 tofu slices. Serve with whole wheat bread.

Per serving: 225 calories; 11 g protein; 13 g fat; 18 g carb; 5 g fiber.

Salmon Pasta with Spicy Tomato Sauce

After reading an article on how to make the most of your money at a salad bar, I learned that you get more for your money by spending it on protein. I developed this recipe using poached salmon from the salad bar. It has become one of my family's favorites. You can also use a leftover salmon fillet from a previous dinner. The red tomato sauce and pink salmon contrast with the dark green pasta to make an elegant dish.

Serves 4

8 ounces spinach fettuccine pasta
1 teaspoon plus 2 tablespoons olive oil
1 cup finely diced red onion
½ teaspoon crushed red pepper flakes
1 teaspoon dried oregano
1 (8-ounce) salmon fillet, precooked
¼ teaspoon dried dill
1 pound Roma tomatoes, peeled, seeded, and chopped
¼ cup dry white wine
Salt and pepper to taste
2 tablespoons chopped fresh parsley, to garnish
¼ cup grated Parmesan cheese, to garnish

Cook pasta in boiling water according to package directions. Drain, reserving pasta water. Toss pasta with 1 teaspoon olive oil. Keep it warm.

Heat 2 tablespoons olive oil in a chef's pan or wok over medium heat. Add onions. Cook and stir until softened. Add red pepper flakes, oregano, and salmon. Break up salmon with a spatula as it cooks. Stir in dill, chopped tomatoes, and wine, and bring to a boil. Turn heat to low. Simmer for 10 minutes, and season with salt and pepper. Add some reserved pasta water if the sauce gets dry. Mound pasta on plates. Make a well in the center of each mound and ladle in the tomato-salmon sauce. Garnish with parsley and Parmesan cheese. Serve warm.

Per serving: 402 calories; 26 g protein; 14 g fat; 41 g carb; 2 g fiber.

Spicy Thai-style Cabbage Salad with Garlic Shrimp

After a trip to Thailand, I came up with this recipe. It has become one of my family's favorite meals. When I served it at one of my dinner parties, a friend told me she was surprised that her young children willingly ate vegetables for the first time! To make a filling and satisfying meal, serve with cooked oats or barley, which are both high in protein and have a low glycemic index.

Serves 4

Simple Thai Dressing
1½ tablespoons fish sauce
2 tablespoons fresh lime juice
½ cup rice milk
1 tablespoon unsweetened shredded
  baking coconut or coconut-milk powder

1 small white or red cabbage, shredded
  (about 4 cups)
3 tablespoons olive oil
½ tablespoon minced fresh ginger
3 garlic cloves, minced
2 fresh red chiles, finely cut into
  thin strips
½ pound raw medium shrimp, peeled
  and deveined
3 tablespoons coarsely chopped roasted
  peanuts, to garnish

Combine dressing ingredients in a bowl. Whisk well, cover, and refrigerate.

In a large pot, bring 5 cups water to a boil. Blanch cabbage for 1 minute. Drain well and put cabbage in a salad bowl.

Heat oil in a nonstick skillet or wok over medium-high heat. Add ginger, garlic, and chiles, and stir-fry until garlic is lightly browned, about 2 minutes. Add shrimp, and stir-fry until they turn opaque, about 2 minutes. Remove from heat.

Mix dressing and shrimp mixture with salad. Toss well. Sprinkle with peanuts. Serve warm with cooked oats or barley (see grain cooking guide on page 17).

Per serving: 257 calories; 16 g protein; 17 g fat; 13 g carb; 3 g fiber.

Orange Beef with Broccoli

Broccoli is high in antioxidants. Oranges are high in vitamins C and A. Together they help strengthen the immune system to combat invasive infections, colds, and flu. If you are in a hurry, use your favorite bottled sauce and precut broccoli.

Serves 4

Orange Sauce

¾ cup fresh orange juice
2 tablespoons soy sauce
1 tablespoon rice wine or dry sherry
½ tablespoon cornstarch
⅛ teaspoon crushed red pepper

2 tablespoons extra-virgin olive oil, divided
2 tablespoons minced fresh ginger
2 tablespoons grated orange zest
1 pound precut stir-fry beef or beef sirloin, trimmed and sliced against the grain into ⅛-inch-thick slices
4 cups broccoli florets

Combine sauce ingredients in a small bowl and stir; set aside.

Heat 1 tablespoon oil in a chef's pan or wok over high heat. Add ginger and orange zest; stir-fry until fragrant, about 30 seconds. Add beef and stir-fry until no longer pink on the outside, about 1 minute. Transfer to a plate and set aside.

Add remaining 1 tablespoon oil to the pan and heat until hot. Add broccoli and stir-fry for 3 minutes or until crisp-tender. Add spicy orange sauce, stirring occasionally, until sauce has thickened slightly, about 2 minutes. Add reserved beef and toss to coat with sauce; heat through. Serve with brown rice or barley (see grain cooking guide on page 17).

Per serving: 344 calories; 27 g protein; 20 g fat; 14 g carb; 3 g fiber.

Stir-fried Black Rice with Green Onions and Ham

Black rice has a nutty taste and soft texture. You can find it at health food stores or gourmet shops, or substitute it with brown rice. You can also substitute ham with smoked salmon or flavored tofu if you wish.

Serves 4

2 large eggs, lightly beaten
1 tablespoon bottled chili garlic sauce or soy sauce
2 teaspoons sesame oil
1 green onion, sliced
1 tablespoon extra-virgin olive oil
¼ pound ham, cut into ½-inch cubes
¼ cup green peas, fresh or frozen
1½ cups cooked black or brown rice
Low-sodium soy sauce, to taste
2 green onions, white part only, sliced, to garnish

In a bowl, beat eggs, chili sauce, and sesame oil until well mixed. Stir in green onion. Set aside.

Heat oil in a nonstick skillet or wok over medium-high heat, and swirl pan to coat it with oil. Pour in egg mixture. Cook without stirring until egg is softly set. Break up egg with a spatula. Add ham, peas, and cooked rice. Cook, stirring, until rice mixture is heated through. Season with soy sauce. Garnish with sliced green onions. Serve hot.

Per serving: 226 calories; 12 g protein; 11 g fat; 19 g carb; 2 g fiber.

Pasta with Spinach, Pine Nuts, and Olives

In this pasta dish, pine nuts and olives provide a nourishing source of protein while adding amazing flavor. Olives have a high content of monounsaturated fatty acids and antioxidants. Studies have shown that olive oil offers protection against heart disease by controlling LDL ("bad" cholesterol) levels while raising HDL ("good" cholesterol) levels.

Serves 4

1 pound penne or fusilli pasta
½ cup dry-pack sun-dried tomatoes
5 tablespoons olive oil, divided
4 garlic cloves, chopped
1 pound fresh baby spinach, washed and drained
½ cup chopped pitted black olives
3 tablespoons balsamic vinegar
¼ cup freshly grated Parmesan cheese
Salt and pepper to taste
½ cup pine nuts, toasted, to garnish
Shaved Parmesan cheese, to garnish

Bring a large pot of water to a boil. Cook pasta according to package directions. Drain. While preparing pasta, rehydrate sun-dried tomatoes in hot water for about 10 minutes, or until plump, then cut into thin strips.

Heat 3 tablespoons oil in a large nonstick skillet or wok over medium heat. Sauté garlic until fragrant. Add spinach. Cook, stirring, for 1 minute, until wilted.

Transfer pasta to a warmed serving bowl. Toss with olives, sun-dried tomatoes, spinach, 2 tablespoons oil, balsamic vinegar, and grated Parmesan cheese. Season with salt and pepper. Garnish with pine nuts and shaved Parmesan cheese.

Per serving: 343 calories; 10 g protein; 23 g fat; 28 g carb; 3 g fiber.

Stir-fried Chicken with Fresh Vegetables and Ginger-Orange Sauce

This is one of my family's favorite weeknight dinners. We serve it over brown rice or whole wheat linguine. If you plan ahead and marinate the chicken overnight, it takes just a few minutes to prepare this dish, making it ideal for a busy evening.

Serves 4–6

Ginger-Orange Sauce

½ cup freshly squeezed orange juice
2 tablespoons rice vinegar
¼ cup soy sauce
2 tablespoons olive oil
1 tablespoon minced fresh ginger
1 green onion, minced

4 tablespoons cornstarch
1 pound skinless chicken breast, cut into long match-size strips
3 tablespoons extra-virgin olive oil
1 tablespoon shredded fresh ginger
1 cup thinly shredded fresh shiitake or portobello mushroom caps
½ cup thinly shredded leeks, white part only
1 cup thinly shredded peeled carrots
Salt and pepper to taste

To prepare sauce, combine all ingredients in a glass jar and mix thoroughly. (This sauce can be stored in the refrigerator for up to a week.)

Combine ½ cup of sauce with cornstarch in a medium-size bowl. Add chicken, cover, and refrigerate for at least 15 minutes or overnight.

Drain off and discard extra sauce from chicken before cooking. Heat oil in a wok or skillet over high heat. Add ginger. Sauté until fragrant, about 30 seconds. Add chicken and stir-fry until no pink remains, 1–2 minutes. Add mushrooms, leeks, and carrots to the skillet. Stir in remaining sauce. Turn down heat and cook, stirring, until vegetables are crisp-tender and heated through, about 1 minute. Season with salt and pepper.

Per serving: 263 calories; 28 g protein; 8 g fat; 18 g carb; 2 g fiber.

Meals in a Pot

During my childhood in China, I would always wait impatiently while my grandmother cooked her delicious stew. She spent hours washing and chopping up the ingredients and cooking the broth. When she finally put all the ingredients in the pot, I would rush to set the table, because I knew that was the final — and quickest — step.

Today I feel so fortunate to have the conveniences of modern life. By using such handy products as organic broth, precut and washed vegetables, and deli meats, I can quickly cook a delicious stew that would have taken my grandmother hours to make. The best part is that it tastes just as delicious as those I remember, and the only cooking equipment I need is a single pot, leaving minimal cleanup afterwards.

Spicy Edamame-Bean Stew

After tasting a Moroccan bean soup at a restaurant, I decided to develop my own variation, adding edamame for an Asian touch. The fiery Middle Eastern spices nicely complement the mild edamame. This stew is a great choice when, at the end of the week, you're low on fresh ingredients. The beans provide a great source of protein. Feel free to choose types of beans that are to your liking.

Serves 4

2 tablespoons extra-virgin olive oil
1 large onion, chopped
2 teaspoons Moroccan Spice Blend
    (or ½ teaspoon ground cinnamon,
    1½ teaspoons ground cumin,
    ⅛ teaspoon cayenne pepper,
    and ½ teaspoon paprika)
1 (15-ounce) can cannellini beans, rinsed
    and drained
1 (15-ounce) can chickpeas, rinsed and
    drained
1 cup frozen edamame
1 (14.5-ounce) can chopped tomatoes
2 (14-ounce) cans vegetable broth or
    reduced-sodium chicken broth
2 cups water
Salt and pepper to taste
¼ cup chopped fresh cilantro, to garnish

Heat oil in a large, heavy pot over medium-high heat. Add onion and sauté for 3 minutes or until softened and translucent. Add spices, beans, chickpeas, and edamame. Cook and stir until aromatic, about 1 minute. Stir in chopped tomatoes, broth, and water. Cover and bring to a boil. Lower to a simmer and cook, partially covered, for about 10 minutes, stirring occasionally to prevent sticking, or until edamame have softened.

Season with salt and pepper. Garnish with cilantro and serve hot with toasted whole wheat bread or flatbread.

Per serving: 389 calories; 18 g protein; 10 g fat; 60 g carb; 14 g fiber.

Baby Back Rib and Daikon Soup with Spicy Soy-Sesame Dipping Sauce

A daikon, also known as a Japanese radish, has a sweet, peppery taste and looks like an oversized white carrot. Look for daikons that are firm and have bright, smooth skin. Avoid those that are soft and wrinkled.

Although this recipe can take a while to cook, preparations are very simple and short. You can either use a slow cooker or simmer the dish on a stove. Either way requires a minimal amount of attention. If you have a pressure cooker, you can cook this soup in less than 30 minutes.

Serves 6

2 pounds baby back ribs, ribs separated
4 ½-inch-thick fresh ginger slices
2 fresh or dried whole red chiles
3 small daikons (about 1 pound), peeled and cut diagonally into 2½-inch chunks
Salt and white pepper to taste

Spicy Soy-Sesame Dipping Sauce
¼ cup low-sodium soy sauce
2 tablespoons rice vinegar or balsamic vinegar
1 small fresh red chile pepper, minced
3 garlic cloves, minced
1 tablespoon black or white sesame seeds, toasted

Rinse ribs under cool running water. Place ribs, ginger, chile peppers, and 7 cups water in a large, heavy pot and bring to a boil. Skim brown foam from the top, add daikons, and return to a boil. Cover, and simmer for 1 hour or until ribs are tender. Season with salt and pepper.

If you use a slow cooker, place ribs, ginger, chile peppers, and 7 cups water in slow cooker and cook on high for 1 hour. Skim brown foam from the top, add daikon, and cook for another 2 hours.

Combine ingredients for dipping sauce and divide into 6 small bowls. Divide broth, ribs, and daikon in 6 shallow bowls and serve with dipping sauce on the side. Serve hot with toasted whole wheat bread.

Per serving: 304 calories; 33 g protein; 14 g fat; 12 g carb; 3 g fiber.

Curried Coconut Pumpkin-Chicken Stew

The pumpkin will absorb the stunning flavors of this delicious broth, and the jalapeño and ginger add more spark to this richly flavored stew. To cut down the fat of the traditional version of this dish, I replace part of the coconut milk with rice milk. It tastes just as delicious. You can substitute the pumpkin with squash or young carrots.

Serves 6–8

2 tablespoons olive oil
¼ cup minced red onion
4 cloves garlic, minced
1 jalapeño pepper, ribs and seeds removed, finely chopped
1 teaspoon minced fresh ginger
2 teaspoons curry powder
1 pound boneless, skinless chicken breasts, cut into 1-inch chunks
1½ cups light coconut milk
1½ cups rice milk
1½ cups peeled, seeded pumpkin, cut into 1-inch cubes
1 red bell pepper, ribs and seeds discarded, cut into 1-inch cubes
1 tablespoon fresh lemon juice
Salt and pepper to taste
¼ cup fresh cilantro leaves, to garnish

Heat oil in a large, heavy pot over medium-high heat. Add onion, garlic, jalapeño, and ginger. Sauté for about 1 minute, or until fragrant. Add curry powder and chicken. Cook and stir for 2 minutes. Stir in coconut milk, rice milk, and pumpkin, and bring to a boil. Lower to a simmer, cover, and cook for 15 minutes or until pumpkin is tender. Add more milk if needed.

Add red bell pepper. Simmer for another 3 minutes, uncovered. Season with lemon juice, salt, and pepper. Garnish with whole cilantro leaves. Serve hot over brown rice or with whole-grain bread.

Per serving: 285 calories; 20 g protein; 19 g fat; 10 g carb; 1 g fiber.

Pork Green Chili

This thick stew is simple to prepare. It gets a delicious boost from oregano and cumin powder. Its wonderful, robust aroma will bring everyone to the table. To save time, I use roasted, skinned chile peppers from the deli or out of the can, as directed below. The stew also stores well in the refrigerator for easy reheating. If you prefer a vegetarian version, simply substitute tofu for the pork.

Serves 4

1 tablespoon olive oil
1 large onion
4 garlic cloves
1 pound pork tenderloin,
    cut into 1-inch cubes
1 tablespoon dried oregano
1 tablespoon cumin powder
2 (14-ounce) cans chicken broth
2 medium tomatoes, chopped
2 (7-ounce) cans whole green chiles,
    drained and chopped
Salt and black pepper to taste
¼ cup chopped fresh cilantro, to garnish

Heat oil in a large, heavy pot over medium-high heat. Add onion and garlic and sauté for 2 minutes or until aromatic. Add pork, oregano, and cumin to pot, and sauté for 2–3 minutes. Pour in broth and tomatoes. Bring to a boil.

Stir and reduce heat. Partially cover and simmer for 25 minutes. Stir in green chiles and simmer for 5 more minutes or until meat is tender. Season with salt and pepper. Garnish with cilantro. Serve hot with whole wheat tortillas or tortilla chips.

Per serving: 251 calories; 31 g protein; 9 g fat; 14 g carb; 5 g fiber.

Beef, Potato, and Carrot Stew

This hearty beef stew makes a lovely dinner on a brisk fall day. The chiles are especially warming, while the turmeric adds an exotic Asian twist. Serve with plenty of crusty bread for mopping up the broth.

Serves 6–8

2 pounds chuck or top-loin New York strip, cut into 1½-inch cubes

2 teaspoons flour

1 teaspoon salt, divided

2 tablespoons extra-virgin olive oil

4 garlic cloves, minced

3 whole chile peppers, fresh or dried

6 cups beef broth or water

1 teaspoon powdered turmeric

1 teaspoon thyme, fresh or dried

1½ teaspoons dill, fresh or dried

1 large red onion, cut into 2-inch wedges

4 medium carrots, peeled and cut diagonally into 2-inch-long chunks

½ pound red potatoes, peeled, cut into 1-inch chunks

1 large Granny Smith apple, peeled, cored, and cut into 1-inch chunks

Toss half of the beef cubes with 1 teaspoon flour and ½ teaspoon salt. Heat 1 tablespoon oil in a large, heavy pot over medium-high heat. Brown beef on all sides, then remove beef from pot. Set all browned beef aside in a bowl. Repeat with remaining beef, flour, ½ teaspoon salt, and oil.

Using the same pot, sauté garlic and chile peppers until fragrant, about 30 seconds. Add beef broth, beef chunks and juices from the bowl, turmeric, thyme, and dill. Cook, stirring, for 2 minutes. Add onion and carrots. Cook, stirring, for 2 minutes. Bring to a boil. Reduce heat to a simmer and cover. Cook for 1 hour. Add potatoes and apple chunks, and cook for 30 minutes more, uncovered, or until meat is tender and broth has thickened.

Per serving: 432 calories; 48 g protein; 17 g fat; 21 g carb; 3 g fiber.

Hearty Spinach and Chickpea Soup

To save time, use prewashed, bagged spinach and canned chickpeas with leftover brown rice or barley. You can double the broth and save half for the next day and make a simple meal by adding cooked noodles, tofu, and bagged vegetables to the hot broth.

Serves 4

Chicken-Mushroom Broth

1 tablespoon olive oil

1 medium onion, finely chopped

2 garlic cloves, minced

8 ounces fresh shiitake mushrooms, stems removed, caps thinly sliced (4 cups)

6 cups reduced-sodium chicken or vegetable broth

½ teaspoon dried rosemary, crumbled

2 cups cooked brown rice

1 (15-ounce) can chickpeas, drained and rinsed

2 (5-ounce) bags baby spinach leaves

Coarse salt and ground pepper to taste

½ cup grated Parmesan cheese, to garnish

Heat oil in a large, heavy pot over medium heat. Add onion and cook, stirring frequently. Add garlic and mushrooms and cook, stirring occasionally, until mushrooms are tender, about 5 minutes. Add broth and rosemary and bring to a boil.

Stir cooked rice and chickpeas into broth and return to a boil. Reduce to a simmer, cover, and continue cooking for 5 more minutes to allow flavors to blend.

Stir in spinach and cook, uncovered, until just wilted, about 1 minute. Season with salt and pepper. Garnish with cheese, and serve immediately. Serve hot with toasted whole wheat bread or flatbread.

Per serving: 385 calories; 21 g protein; 9 g fat; 56 g carb; 9 g fiber.

Quinoa with Rotisserie Chicken and Green Peas

This aromatic, protein-rich meal with high-fiber quinoa will delight the whole family. Although store-bought rotisserie chickens are convenient timesavers, some are high in sodium and unhealthy. Look for chickens that are low in sodium but also haven't been treated with antibiotics or hormones. Feel free to substitute the rotisserie chicken with leftover chicken or turkey (this can be a great simple meal for the weekend after Thanksgiving!).

Serves 4

2 (14-ounce) cans low-sodium chicken broth

1½ tablespoons soy sauce

1 tablespoon rice wine or white wine

2 cups cooked quinoa or brown rice (see grain cooking guide on page 17)

1 store-bought organic rotisserie chicken, trimmed, boned, and cut into 2-inch pieces (to make 4 cups)

1½ cups frozen green peas

Salt and white pepper to taste

1 tablespoon toasted sesame oil

¼ cup minced green onions, to garnish

Pour broth into a large, heavy pot, along with soy sauce and wine. Bring to a boil, reduce heat to medium-low, and stir in quinoa and chicken. Cover and simmer for 5–8 minutes, until quinoa and chicken are heated through.

Stir in peas and simmer for 2 minutes or until peas are heated through. Season with salt and pepper. Drizzle with sesame oil and garnish with green onions. Serve hot.

Per serving: 415 calories; 50 g protein; 11 g fat; 30 g carb; 5 g fiber.

Essential Miso Soup with Tofu and Noodles

This is not the light miso soup you taste in restaurants. The dense tofu and whole wheat noodles make this a hearty, warming meal, perfect for a cold, rainy day. Fresh udon noodles work best in this dish, but if you can't find them, use fresh linguine or wide rice noodles.

Serves 4

½ pound udon or soba noodles
4 cups canned vegetable broth
8 ounces flavor-baked tofu, cut into ½-inch cubes
½ cup peeled and thinly sliced carrots
2 tablespoons red miso
2 green onions, minced
1 tablespoon sesame oil
¼ cup mung or soybean sprouts
Low-sodium soy sauce to taste

Cook noodles according to package directions. Drain in a colander under cold running water and set aside.

Bring broth to a boil in a large pot. Add tofu, cooked noodles, and carrots. Bring soup back to a boil. Reduce heat to low and simmer for 3 minutes.

In a small bowl, mash miso with about ¼ cup warm soup until it forms a smooth sauce, then stir mixture back into the soup pot. Turn off heat.

Stir in green onions and sesame oil. Top with sprouts. Season with soy sauce. Serve hot.

Per serving: 185 calories; 11 g protein; 7 g fat; 21 g carb; 2 g fiber.

Crab, Corn, and Red Potato Chowder

This simple yet flavorful chowder is an ideal dish for a cold day. The salty bacon lends a truly magical touch to the creamy, sweet texture. For those who can't eat dairy products, use extra-virgin olive oil and rice milk instead of butter and milk. It's just as delicious and satisfying.

Serves 6

2 tablespoons butter or extra-virgin
   olive oil
2 strips bacon, cut into 1-inch pieces
1 cup chopped onion
1 cup diced celery
1 pound red potatoes, cut into 1-inch
   cubes
3 tablespoons flour
4 cups whole milk or rice milk
2 cups frozen corn kernels
8 ounces fresh or canned crabmeat
Salt and black pepper to taste
2 tablespoons minced fresh parsley

Melt butter or heat oil in a large, heavy pot over medium-high heat. Add bacon, onion, and celery. Sauté for 2 minutes. Add potatoes and sauté for 1 minute. Sprinkle with flour and cook for 1 minute, stirring constantly.

Stir in milk and corn. Bring to a boil over medium-low heat, stirring frequently. Cover, reduce heat, and simmer for 20 minutes or until potatoes are tender.

Stir in crabmeat. Cook for 3 minutes, stirring occasionally. Season with salt and pepper. Garnish with parsley. Serve hot with a toasted baguette or whole-grain crackers.

Per serving: 327 calories; 17 g protein; 17 g fat; 37 g carb; 3 g fiber.

Seafood Stew

Legend has it that seafood stew was first concocted on the docks of San Francisco's Fisherman's Wharf. Fishermen would add something from the day's catch to the communal stew kettle on the wharf, constantly giving the dish a new flavor — kind of like a fisherman's stone soup. Following with the tradition, be creative with this stew. Leave something out, or add something new to your liking. Serve it with a toasted baguette or whole-grain crackers.

Serves 6

3 tablespoons olive oil or butter
3 cloves garlic, minced
2 medium onions, chopped
2 medium tomatoes, chopped
2 (14-ounce) cans fish stock
1 pound raw extra-large shrimp, peeled and deveined
½ pound fish fillets (halibut or cod), cut into about 2-inch chunks
½ pound large scallops
Salt and white pepper to taste
3 tablespoons fresh cilantro leaves or chives, to garnish

Heat oil or butter in a large, heavy pot over medium-high heat. Add garlic and onions, stirring often until onions are soft, about 5 minutes. Add tomatoes and fish stock. Bring to a boil, then stir in shrimp, fish, and scallops.

Reduce heat, cover, and simmer for about 8 minutes or until shrimp are opaque. Season with salt and pepper. Garnish with cilantro or chives. Serve hot.

Per serving: 265 calories; 34 g protein; 10 g fat; 8 g carb; 1 g fiber.

Turkey Curry

~~~~~~

Turkey is low in fat and a healthy alternative to red meat. Although this simple dish is ideal for leftover turkey after the holidays, you can make it year-round by using deli meat and bagged, washed spinach. Turkey is low in fat and a healthy alternative to red meat. Feel free to replace the turkey with tofu and the chicken broth with vegetable broth for a vegetarian version. Serve it with brown rice or barley.

Serves 6

1 tablespoon extra-virgin olive oil
1 large onion, finely chopped
2 teaspoons curry powder
2 (14-ounce) cans chicken broth
½ cup coconut milk
1 pound cooked turkey, cut into
  2-inch cubes
3 cups fresh baby spinach
Salt and pepper to taste
3 tablespoons almond slices, to garnish

Heat oil in a large, heavy pot over medium-high heat. Add onions and curry powder, cook, stirring often, until onions are soft, about 5 minutes. Stir in broth and coconut milk. Bring to a boil. Add turkey, cover, reduce heat, and simmer for about 5 minutes.

Stir in spinach and continue to simmer until heated through, about 2 minutes. Season with salt and pepper. Garnish with almond slices. Serve with brown rice or barley.

Per serving: 323 calories; 39 g protein; 15 g fat; 7 g carb; 2 g fiber.

Meals in a Hurry

When I first came to the United States, I was surprised by how clean the vegetables were in the grocery store, in contrast to the often muddy vegetables in my hometown market. It astonished me when my American host told me that I could eat raw vegetables right from the bag. Since then, my obsession with clean vegetables has inspired me to develop many recipes like the ones in this chapter. All you need is to use your matchmaking skills — to mix and match the ingredients — and in minutes you will be enjoying an enticing, healthy meal.

Couscous with Pine Nuts, Cranberries, and Grapefruit

The colorful presentation of this dish proves that simple food can be visually stunning, delicious, and good for you. Couscous requires a short preparation time. It has a low glycemic load, and is rich in B vitamins. Chickpeas (also called garbanzo beans) are a rich source of vegetable protein and minerals.

Serves 4

1 cup grapefruit juice, freshly squeezed or unsweetened bottled

½ cup couscous

¾ cup canned chickpeas, rinsed and drained

1 green onion, minced

1 small tomato, peeled and diced

2 tablespoons olive oil

3 tablespoons capers

½ medium grapefruit

¼ cup dried cranberries

¼ cup pine nuts, toasted

Salt and pepper to taste

¼ cup chopped fresh basil leaves, to garnish

In a 2-quart saucepan, bring grapefruit juice to a boil. Stir in couscous. Cover saucepan and remove from heat. Let stand until couscous has absorbed all the juice, about 5 minutes.

In a large serving bowl, mix together couscous, chickpeas, green onion, tomato, olive oil, and capers. Toss gently to combine.

Using a paring knife, cut out bite-size sections of grapefruit, leaving behind the membrane. Stir grapefruit chunks, cranberries, and pine nuts into couscous mixture. Season with salt and pepper if needed. Garnish with basil leaves before serving.

Per serving: 366 calories; 7 g protein; 14 g fat; 57 g carb; 6 g fiber.

Garden Salad with Blueberries, Blue Cheese, and Walnuts

~~~~~~

In this eye-pleasing salad, several healthy ingredients are combined in a dish that will appeal to salad lovers of all ages. The tasty sweet walnuts contrast wonderfully with blue cheese, plus walnuts have more omega-3 fatty acids than any other nut. Research has shown that omega-3 prevents heart disease and is essential for healthy skin and cells. The blueberries, a rich source of antioxidants, are often called a superfood. Feel free to substitute other fresh vegetables and berries that are in season.

Serves 4

6 ounces baby-greens salad mix
1 red tomato, sliced into wedges
1 yellow tomato, sliced into wedges
1 cup fresh blueberries
3 tablespoons walnut oil
2 tablespoons balsamic vinegar
Salt and pepper to taste
½ cup blue or Roquefort cheese, crumbled
½ cup candied walnuts, to garnish

In a large salad bowl, gently toss salad greens, tomato wedges, blueberries, walnut oil, vinegar, salt, and pepper. Mix in blue cheese and top with candied walnuts.

Serve with whole wheat bread.

Per serving: 287 calories; 7 g protein; 25 g fat; 11 g carb; 3 g fiber.

Savory Sautéed Tofu and Soybeans

Cranberries and soybeans make this protein-rich recipe a colorful dish that will tempt children and adults alike. Pair up this dish with one of the cooked grains from the chart on page 17, or serve on a bed of noodles. In addition to being a complete protein, soybeans are a rich source of omega-3 fatty acids, fiber, vitamins, and minerals.

Serves 4

1 tablespoon olive oil

1 (8-ounce) package Thai or other flavor baked tofu, cut into 1-inch cubes

2 cups shelled green soybeans

3 green onions, white part only, thinly sliced

½ cup dried cranberries

1 tablespoon soy sauce

1 tablespoon fresh lemon juice

2 teaspoons sesame oil

Heat a nonstick skillet or wok over medium-high heat. Add oil and swirl pan to coat. Add tofu and stir-fry until golden-brown, about 2 minutes. Add soybeans and stir-fry for 2 minutes or until heated through. Add green onions, cranberries, soy sauce, and lemon juice. Stir-fry until heated through, 1–2 minutes. Drizzle with sesame oil. Serve hot over a bed of rice or noodles.

Per serving: 403 calories; 24 g protein; 23 g fat; 31 g carb; 8 g fiber.

Chicken Waldorf Salad with Flaxseed Oil Dressing

Flaxseed oil is high in heart-healthy omega-3 fats. Better yet, its rich, nutty taste brings out the sweet, tart flavor of apples and cranberries. This is a very quick meal due to the use of rotisserie chicken. Select an organic rotisserie chicken that's low in salt. A large chicken with more than 3 cups of meat can provide leftovers for the next day's meal. Serve with toasted whole wheat bread.

Serves 4

½ cup walnuts
2 tablespoons olive oil
2 tablespoons flaxseed oil
3 tablespoons cider vinegar
1 teaspoon honey
2 tablespoons water
Coarse salt and pepper to taste
2 Granny Smith apples (1 pound total), cored and cut into ¼-inch wedges
½ cup dried cranberries
2 stalks celery, thinly sliced
½ small onion, finely chopped
3 cups (12 ounces) thickly shredded skinless rotisserie chicken (from 1 small chicken)

Preheat oven to 350°F. Toast walnuts on a dry sheet pan until crisp and fragrant, about 10 minutes. When cool enough to handle, chop coarsely, and set aside.

In a large bowl, whisk together olive oil, flaxseed oil, vinegar, honey, and water. Season to taste with salt and pepper. Add apples, dried cranberries, celery, onion, and chicken. Toss to combine. Divide salad among 4 plates, and top each serving with walnuts.

Per serving: 467 calories; 27 g protein; 26 g fat; 35 g carb; 5 g fiber.

Annatto Rice with Sausage and Tomato

Once you master this highly flavorful and satisfying dish, you can make it one of your go-to recipes. It can be easily doubled or tripled for parties or a potluck. Reminiscent of saffron but less expensive, annatto seeds can be found in Latin grocery stores. Sautéing the annatto seeds lends a warm, yellow hue to the dish. Grapeseed oil is rich in HDL ("good" cholesterol) and helps lower LDL ("bad" cholesterol). If you don't have any on hand, you can substitute it with olive oil.

Serves 4

3 tablespoons grapeseed oil

1½ tablespoons annatto seeds

1 small red chile, stemmed, seeded, and minced

3 cloves garlic, minced

½ pound vegetarian or organic chicken sausages, cut into bite-size pieces

1 cup diced tomatoes

4 small bay leaves, broken in half

2 cups cooked long-grain white rice

Salt and freshly ground black pepper to taste

In a medium sauté pan, heat oil and annatto seeds over medium heat until sizzling. Lower temperature and cook until oil turns yellow, about 3 minutes. Turn off heat. Using a slotted spoon, remove annatto seeds and discard.

Reheat annatto oil over medium-high heat. Add chile and garlic, stir, and sauté for 30 seconds. Add sausage, tomato, and bay leaves. Cook, stirring, until heated through. Stir in cooked rice. Remove and discard bay leaves. Season with salt and pepper. Serve warm.

Per serving: 373 calories; 14 g protein; 21 g fat; 36 g carb; 4 g fiber.

Orange-Ginger Lamb Kabobs

To save time, buy precut lamb cubes. If you can, marinate the lamb overnight to let the orange-ginger marinade tenderize the meat. To give these kabobs a juicy twist, use fresh orange. You can also use other fresh firm fruit in place of orange, such as pineapple, mango, or peaches. The delicious orange-ginger sauce also pairs well with other grilled meats, seafood, and tofu. If you use bamboo skewers, soak them in cold water before using them, to reduce scorching.

Serves 4

Orange-Ginger Marinade
½ cup fresh orange juice
  (about 2 oranges)
2 tablespoons minced green onions
1 tablespoon minced fresh ginger
1 tablespoon minced fresh cilantro
2 tablespoons rice vinegar
2 tablespoons low-sodium soy sauce
1 minced red chile (optional)

1 pound lamb, cubed
1 large sweet onion
2 large navel oranges

To make marinade, combine orange juice, green onions, ginger, cilantro, vinegar, soy sauce, and chile (if using) in a bowl. Add lamb; toss to coat. Cover and marinate in refrigerator for at least 15 minutes, or overnight.

Peel and cut onion and oranges into eight wedges; halve each wedge. Oil grill rack with cooking spray. Preheat grill to high.

Remove lamb from dish. Discard marinade. Alternately thread lamb, orange wedges, and onion wedges onto eight metal or soaked wooden skewers. Grill, covered, over medium-high heat for 8–10 minutes or until meat is desired doneness, and onions are crisp-tender. Serve with couscous.

Per serving: 388 calories; 21 g protein; 26 g fat; 18 g carb; 3 g fiber.

Roma Tomato Salad with Feta and Garlic

This recipe is my family's go-to dish on hot summer days. It reminds me of the hot summers in Wuhan, when my grandmother often served tomato salad. By adding feta for protein and serving it with whole wheat crackers or bread, the salad becomes a complete meal.

Serves 4

8 Roma tomatoes, cut into wedges

4 cloves garlic, minced finely (or sliced)

½ cup fresh basil leaves cut into thin strips

3 tablespoons olive oil

2 tablespoons balsamic vinegar

4 ounces tomato-basil or plain feta, crumbled or sliced

In a large bowl, toss together tomatoes, garlic, basil, olive oil, balsamic vinegar, and feta cheese. Chill in refrigerator for 10 minutes before serving.

Per serving: 198 calories; 5 g protein; 16 g fat; 8 g carb; 2 g fiber.

Garlic-Cilantro Pesto with Sun-dried Tomatoes on White Fish Fillets

Pesto is traditionally made with fresh basil, which can be hard to find in the winter. This recipe calls for cilantro, but feel free to use fresh basil when it's available. Cilantro can quickly lose its flavor and become harsh-tasting, so use it shortly after buying.

Serves 4

Garlic-Cilantro Pesto

¼ cup toasted walnuts, crushed

1–3 cloves garlic, crushed

1¼ cups fresh cilantro leaves

2 tablespoons (about 1 ounce) chopped dry-pack sun-dried tomatoes

1½ tablespoons olive oil

1 tablespoon white wine vinegar

2 tablespoons freshly grated Parmesan cheese

½ teaspoon minced fresh chile pepper

Salt to taste

2 pounds cod or other firm white fish fillets, cut into 4 portions

Salt and pepper to taste

1 tablespoon extra-virgin olive oil

To make pesto, combine walnuts, garlic, cilantro, sun-dried tomatoes, oil, vinegar, Parmesan, and chile pepper in a food processor or blender. Puree until smooth, adding more oil if needed, until pesto reaches your desired consistency. Season with salt.

Season fish on both sides with salt and pepper. Heat oil in a large nonstick skillet over medium-high heat. Add fish and cook until golden, about 2 minutes per side.

Garnish each fish portion with ½ cup pesto. Serve over whole wheat or soba (buckwheat) noodles.

Per serving: 324 calories; 43 g protein; 14 g fat; 6 g carb; 1 g fiber.

Orange-Spinach Salad with Sunflower Seeds and Cranberries

~~~~~~

Spice up healthy spinach leaves with this tasty combination of sweet and tangy flavors. While it's good for dinner on a hot summer day, the sunflower seeds and cranberries make this salad a year-round favorite. Not only are sunflower seeds rich in vitamins and minerals, they are a great source of cholesterol-lowering phytosterols. If you don't have sunflower seeds on hand, feel free to substitute with another small or chopped nut.

Serves 4

¼ cup olive oil
2 thick slices whole wheat bread
¼ cup brown sugar
½ cup sunflower seeds
1 large orange
1 pound baby spinach leaves, washed and dried
2 tablespoons balsamic vinegar
¼ cup dried cranberries

Coat a nonstick skillet with ½ tablespoon oil. Pan-fry bread on one side until golden brown, about 2–3 minutes. Remove bread, recoat pan with another ½ tablespoon oil, and pan-fry other side of bread until golden brown. Cut bread into ½-inch cubes. Drain on paper towels.

Lay out a sheet of aluminum foil. In a small sauté pan, heat 1 tablespoon oil over medium-low heat. Add brown sugar and stir until it melts. Add sunflower seeds and mix until well coated. Pour onto aluminum foil and break up pieces with a fork. Allow seeds to cool.

Peel orange, separate wedges, and cut wedges into bite-size pieces. Place spinach in a salad bowl. Mix in vinegar and remaining oil. Toss, add orange pieces and cranberries, and mix gently. Top with sunflower seeds and bread cubes.

Per serving: 380 calories; 9 g protein; 23 g fat; 41 g carb; 7 g fiber.

Grilled Salmon with Spicy Honey-Basil Sauce

This is a simple and delicious way to cook salmon that requires very little hands-on time. To truly make it a meal in a hurry, plan ahead and marinate the fish the night before you plan to eat it. If you don't have time to make the sauce, substitute with your favorite bottled sauce.

Serves 4

Spicy Honey-Basil Sauce
2 tablespoons pine nuts, toasted
1 tablespoon honey
2 tablespoons fresh lemon juice
¼ cup olive oil
½ cup packed fresh basil leaves
2 cloves garlic, minced
1 small red chile pepper or 1 medium jalapeño, chopped (include seeds if you like it spicy)

4 (4-ounce) skinless salmon fillets
¼ cup diced red bell pepper
¼ cup diced yellow bell pepper
¼ cup chopped watercress leaves
1 tablespoon balsamic vinegar
1 tablespoon olive oil
Salt and ground white pepper to taste

To prepare sauce, place pine nuts, honey, lemon juice, olive oil, basil, garlic, and chile in a blender or food processor. Process until mixture is pureed. Spoon sauce over salmon, and turn to coat. Cover and refrigerate overnight or for at least 4 hours, turning twice.

Place bell peppers and watercress in a bowl. Toss with vinegar and olive oil. Cover and refrigerate while salmon cooks.

Oil grill rack and preheat grill to medium-high. Remove salmon from sauce, reserving the sauce. Sprinkle salmon with salt and pepper on both sides. Place salmon on grill rack and grill until opaque throughout, 4–6 minutes on each side. Occasionally brush with reserved sauce.

Garnish salmon with bell pepper and watercress mixture and serve with brown rice.

Per serving: 324 calories; 20 g protein; 23 g fat; 9 g carb; 1 g fiber.

Asparagus and Crab Salad

Use young, tender asparagus for this salad. To keep asparagus fresh, place the stalks upright in a tall container with 2 inches of water. Keep in a cool place or the refrigerator. Change the water daily. Serve this healthy salad with thick slices of fresh whole grain bread, and use the bread to soak up the delicious sauce.

Serves 4

½ pound cooked lump crabmeat or canned
½ tablespoon rice wine
1 tablespoon soy sauce
1½ tablespoons fresh lemon juice
1 Thai chile, finely minced
1 green onion, minced
1 pound thin asparagus spears, woody ends removed, cut into 1-inch lengths
¼ cup chopped honey-roasted nuts of your choice, to garnish

Combine crabmeat, rice wine, soy sauce, lemon juice, chile, and green onion.

Blanch asparagus pieces in a large saucepan of boiling salted water until bright green, about 1 minute. Drain and rinse with cold water until chilled.

Toss asparagus and crabmeat mixture in a salad bowl. Top with nuts and serve.

Per serving: 185 calories; 24 g protein; 6 g fat; 9 g carb; 4 g fiber.

Spicy Sesame Pad Thai

In this savory dish, the wide, silken rice noodles absorb the spicy, slightly sweet sesame sauce. To save time on a weeknight, make the sauce in advance; it will last up to a week when refrigerated in a sealed container. It also goes well with other types of noodles.

Serves 4

Spicy Sesame Sauce

½ tablespoon extra-virgin olive oil
1 garlic clove, minced
2–3 fresh chile peppers, such as jalapeño or serrano, seeded and minced
¼ cup sesame tahini
¼ cup soy milk
½ tablespoon fresh lemon juice

8 ounces wide rice noodles, fresh or dry
1 tablespoon olive oil
1 cup julienned red bell peppers
1 cup julienned green onions
Salt and pepper to taste
2 tablespoons toasted sesame seeds, to garnish

To prepare sauce, in a small saucepan, heat oil over medium heat. Add garlic and chile peppers and sauté for 1 minute. Add tahini, soy milk, and lemon juice. Cook, stirring constantly, until sauce is hot and tahini has melted, 1–2 minutes. Remove from heat and let cool.

Cook noodles according to package directions. Drain and rinse with cold water to prevent sticking. Set aside.

Heat oil in a nonstick skillet over medium-high heat. Add bell peppers and green onions, and stir-fry for 30 seconds. Stir in noodles and sesame sauce. Season with salt and pepper. Transfer to serving dish. Garnish with sesame seeds.

Per serving: 399 calories; 7 g protein; 16 g fat; 58 g carb; 5 g fiber.

Global Inspiration

I love to eat and travel. Everywhere I go, I spend hours searching for good food. The dishes I enjoy the most are those that feature fresh ingredients and flavorful spices. Once I get home, I eagerly go to my kitchen to re-create the dishes I've discovered, using organic meat and fresh produce from my local market when possible. It's a way of sharing my experiences with my family and friends, giving them a taste of my trip. Some of the best meals are created when I mix and match ingredients from different parts of the world.

Shrimp and Olive Pizza

Experiment with other shellfish and seafood, such as mussels, crabmeat, smoked salmon, and calamari. For a nontraditional pizza sauce, replace tomato sauce with sun-dried tomato pesto sauce.

Serves 4

1 (11-ounce) package prepared pizza
  dough
2 tablespoons cornmeal
½ cup organic pizza sauce
4 ounces crumbled feta cheese
¾ cup sliced fresh basil leaves
2 firm, medium-size tomatoes, thinly
  sliced
15 small pitted black olives, sliced in half
15 small pitted green olives, sliced in half
½ pound cooked large shrimp, peeled
  and deveined

Preheat oven to 475°F. Pat dough out into a flat circle on a lightly floured surface. With a rolling pin, roll it out to the size of a pizza pan or round baking pan. Sprinkle cornmeal onto pan and place pizza dough on it.

Spread pizza sauce over pizza dough, leaving rim uncovered. Sprinkle with feta and ½ cup basil. Arrange tomato slices evenly over cheese. Artistically arrange black and green olives on top. Bake for 12 minutes or until crust is light golden brown on the edges and cheese has melted.

Remove pizza from oven. Arrange shrimp among olives. Return pizza to oven and bake for 3 more minutes. Remove from oven, sprinkle with remaining sliced basil, and serve.

Per serving: 384 calories; 24 g protein; 12 g fat; 46 g carb; 4 g fiber.

Linguine and Tuna with Spicy Orange Sauce

Look for canned West Coast hook-and-line or troll-caught albacore tuna (available at many natural food stores). The fish tend to be smaller and contain less mercury and more omega-3 "good" fats than the larger, deep-sea albacore used in most cans. Otherwise, choose "light" tuna, which also has low mercury levels.

Serves 4

8 ounces whole wheat linguine
1½ teaspoons grated orange zest
¾ cup fresh orange juice
   (from 2–3 oranges)
3 tablespoons olive oil
2 tablespoons balsamic vinegar
2 tablespoons Dijon mustard
1 teaspoon red pepper flakes
   (plus more for garnish)
Salt to taste
1 large bunch watercress, tough ends
   trimmed, washed and well dried
   (about 3 cups)
2 (6-ounce) cans tuna packed in oil,
   drained

In a large pot of boiling water, cook pasta according to package instructions; drain.

Meanwhile, in a large bowl, whisk together orange zest, orange juice, oil, vinegar, mustard, and red pepper flakes. Season with salt. Add watercress and pasta, and toss to combine. Scatter tuna over top of pasta, sprinkle with red pepper flakes (if desired), and serve.

Per serving: 366 calories; 29 g protein; 18 g fat; 22 g carb; 3 g fiber.

Smoked Salmon-Chile Pepper Omelet

In this recipe, I season the eggs with soy sauce, smoked salmon, and sesame oil before cooking, which makes it much more flavorful than your typical omelet. Let the oil heat up before pouring in the egg mixture; this will allow the eggs to fluff up as they cook. You can test the oil with a small drop of egg. If the drop immediately starts to cook, then it is hot enough. A 9-inch nonstick omelet or sauté pan will work best for this recipe.

Serves 4

5 organic eggs
2 teaspoons sesame oil
1 tablespoon soy sauce
2 green onions, green part only, minced
3 ounces smoked salmon, minced
1 red chile pepper, seeded and finely minced
2 medium mushrooms, minced
Salt and white pepper to taste
4 tablespoons sunflower oil

In a large bowl, whisk eggs, sesame oil, and soy sauce until frothy. Stir in green onions, smoked salmon, chile pepper, mushrooms, salt, and white pepper.

Heat 3 tablespoons sunflower oil in a 9-inch nonstick pan over medium heat. Swirl pan to coat. Pour in egg mixture. Cook until edges of omelet have solidified, about 2 minutes. With a spatula, lift edges of omelet so uncooked egg runs underneath. Continue cooking without stirring until omelet is almost firm on top and browned underneath, about 2–3 minutes.

Slide omelet onto a heatproof plate. Add remaining tablespoon of sunflower oil to pan, then carefully flip omelet back into pan and brown the other side. Cut it in wedges to serve hot or at room temperature.

Per serving: 285 calories; 16 g protein; 24 g fat; 3 g carb; 1 g fiber.

Orange Quinoa and Sweet Potato Salad

Quinoa, a South America grain, is rich in magnesium and is a complete protein, meaning it contains all nine essential amino acids. Just like tofu, quinoa takes on the flavor of whatever you cook it with. After soaking up the juice of the oranges, it nicely accompanies the sweet potatoes and crunchy nuts. Quinoa is available in the natural foods sections of many supermarkets. Always rinse it before cooking to remove any residue saponins.

Serves 4

1 cup organic quinoa
2 cups water
1 medium sweet potato
3 tablespoons fresh orange juice
2 tablespoons olive oil
2 tablespoons fresh lemon juice
½ teaspoon salt
¼ teaspoon freshly ground black pepper
2 large oranges, peeled and cut into
  8 wedges
1 cup chopped spinach

¼ cup chopped walnuts, to garnish
1 orange cut into rings, to garnish

Rinse quinoa thoroughly. Meanwhile, bring water to a boil. Add quinoa, cover, reduce heat to a simmer, and cook until quinoa is tender and all water is absorbed, about 15 minutes. Remove from heat and let cool.

Place sweet potato in a large baking dish; pierce with a knife. Microwave on high heat until soft, about 8–10 minutes. Peel and cut into 3-inch pieces.

In a large bowl, whisk orange juice, oil, lemon juice, salt, and pepper. Add quinoa, sweet potato, orange wedges, and spinach. Toss to combine. Divide salad among 4 bowls, top with nuts, and garnish with orange rings.

Per serving: 265 calories; 5 g protein; 13 g fat; 36 g carb; 6 g fiber.

Pan-seared Salmon with Lemon-Dill Yogurt Sauce

The cooling yogurt sauce balances the pan-seared salmon. For a slightly sweet version, add a few tablespoons of freshly squeezed orange juice to the yogurt sauce.

Serves 4

Lemon-Dill Yogurt Sauce
1 cup plain soy or regular yogurt
2 tablespoons chopped fresh dillweed
2 teaspoons lemon zest
1 tablespoon extra-virgin olive oil

1 tablespoon butter
4 (4-ounce) skinless salmon fillets
1 tablespoon extra-virgin olive oil
3 cloves garlic, finely chopped
2 cups cooked mixed fresh vegetables or thawed frozen mixed vegetables
Salt and pepper to taste

In a medium bowl, combine yogurt, dill, lemon zest, and oil. Mix well and set aside.

In a large sauté pan, melt butter on medium-high heat. Add salmon fillets and sear for about 3 minutes. Turn fillets over and cook for about 3 more minutes or until salmon flakes with a fork. Place fish on a warm serving plate.

Heat oil and sauté garlic until fragrant. Add vegetables and sauté until heated through. Season with salt and pepper.

To serve, arrange vegetables around salmon fillets and spoon yogurt sauce over fillets. Serve warm with couscous.

Per serving: 340 calories; 35 g protein; 16 g fat; 14 g carb; 3 g fiber.

Paprika Shrimp with Turnips and Walnuts

Shrimp is a good source of protein that is low in saturated fat and calories. It is also a good source of vitamin D, vitamin B12, and selenium, an antioxidant. It takes only minutes to cook, so shrimp makes an ideal choice for busy weeknight meals.

For Westerners, turnips are an unusual choice for stir-fry, but are common in Asian dishes. They are a good source of fiber, vitamins, and calcium. Feel free to substitute daikons or carrots for the turnips. Serve over whole wheat pasta or brown rice.

Serves 4

2–3 tablespoons olive oil

1 tablespoon minced fresh ginger

½ tablespoon paprika

3 tablespoons chopped walnuts

1 pound raw large shrimp, peeled and deveined

1½ cups quarter-inch-cubed washed turnips

1 tablespoon balsamic or sherry vinegar

3 tablespoons sake or rice wine

Salt and pepper to taste

¼ cup chopped fresh parsley (optional)

Heat oil in a large skillet over medium-high heat. Add ginger and paprika and cook, stirring constantly, until fragrant, about 20 seconds. Add walnuts and sauté until lightly browned.

Add shrimp and cook, stirring, until pink and opaque, about 2 minutes per side. Stir in turnips, vinegar, sake, salt, and pepper. Cook, stirring, until heated through, about 2 minutes. Stir in parsley, if using. Serve warm.

Per serving: 256 calories; 24 g protein; 13 g fat; 7 g carb; 2 g fiber.

Curried Chicken Wraps

Sweet, juicy grapes complement curried chicken in these easy wraps. The filling from India and tortilla wrapper from Central America make this recipe another example of how you can successfully blend elements from East and West. Any leftover filling is delicious, served cold, in a wrap the following day.

Serves 4 (2 wraps each)

8 (10-inch) whole wheat flour tortillas
1 pound boneless, skinless chicken breasts, trimmed
1 tablespoon olive oil
½ cup chopped green onions (1 bunch)
1 tablespoon minced fresh ginger
1 tablespoon freshly grated orange zest
1 tablespoon finely chopped jalapeño or serrano pepper (2 small peppers)
1 teaspoon curry powder
1 tablespoon rice wine, sake, or orange juice
½ teaspoon salt, or to taste
Freshly ground pepper to taste
1½ cups red seedless grapes (8 ounces), washed, dried, and halved
1½ cups low-fat plain yogurt

Preheat oven to 400°F. Wrap tortillas in foil, place in oven, and warm while you prepare filling.

Meanwhile, cut chicken into ¼-inch-thick slices. Turn slices on their sides and cut into ¼-inch-strips. Heat a wok or large nonstick skillet over medium-high heat. Add oil and tilt pan to coat evenly. Add green onions, ginger, orange zest, and jalapeño (or serrano). Cook, stirring, until fragrant, about 1 minute.

Add chicken and stir-fry for 1 minute. Add curry powder, rice wine (or sake or orange juice), salt, and pepper. Cook, stirring, until chicken is browned and no longer pink in the center, about 2 minutes. Transfer to a bowl. Add grapes and toss to mix.

To serve, spoon about ½ cup of chicken filling into each warm tortilla. Top filling with 2 tablespoons yogurt. Roll up tortilla and eat with your fingers. Serve remaining yogurt for dipping.

Per wrap: 307 calories; 14 g protein; 8 g fat; 44 g carb; 1 g fiber.

Baked Tilapia Packages with Roasted Red Pepper and Sun-dried Tomato Sauce

This simple yet elegant dish could be your go-to recipe when you have guests for dinner. The fish is enclosed in parchment paper and baked in sun-dried tomato sauce, a simple and healthy way to prepare fish. To save time, use a store-bought sun-dried tomato sauce, or you can make the sauce a few days in advance. If you can't find small yellow tomatoes, a couple of additional red tomatoes will do.

Serves 4

Roasted Red Pepper and Sun-dried Tomato Sauce

1 cup bottled roasted red bell peppers, drained

¼ cup (about 2 ounces) dry-pack sun-dried tomatoes, chopped

2 cloves garlic

3 tablespoons fresh lemon juice

2 tablespoons balsamic vinegar

4 (3–4 ounce) skinless tilapia fillets

4 small red tomatoes, cut into 1-inch cubes

2 small yellow tomatoes, cut into 1-inch cubes

4 (12-inch) squares parchment paper

½ tablespoon dried parsley

Place sauce ingredients in a blender or food processor and process until smooth. Pour into a container.

Rinse fish fillets under cold water and drain thoroughly in a colander. Place fillets and tomatoes in a bowl. Add ¾ cup sauce and toss lightly to coat. Cover and refrigerate for at least 15 minutes, or overnight for best flavor.

Preheat oven to 450°F. Fold each square of parchment paper (or aluminum foil) in half on the diagonal to create a crease; unfold. Arrange one fish fillet on a square lengthwise, just below the fold. Top fillet with some tomatoes and sauce, and fold paper over to enclose fish completely. Fold and crimp edges of package to seal.

Arrange packages on a cookie sheet. Bake for 10–12 minutes on the middle rack, or until packages puff up and the thickest part of fish flakes easily with a fork. To serve, cut open packages with scissors, and garnish with dried parsley. Serve hot with whole wheat bread.

Per serving: 167 calories; 21 g protein; 2 g fat; 19 g carb; 4 g fiber.

Spicy Bean Soft Tacos

You can make this dish as spicy as you like by varying the amount of chipotle peppers, or by using a spicier salsa. Canned chipotles in adobo can be found in the specialty section of most supermarkets.

Serves 4

8 (7-inch) whole wheat flour tortillas
1 tablespoon olive oil
3 green onions, thinly sliced
2 garlic cloves, minced
2 (15-ounce) cans pinto beans, drained and rinsed
1 canned chipotle pepper in adobo, finely chopped, plus more for serving (optional)
Coarse salt and ground pepper to taste
1 cup store-bought green salsa, plus more for serving (optional)
½ cup frozen corn kernels, thawed
1–2 tablespoons fresh lime juice
½ cup plain low-fat yogurt
½ cup packed fresh cilantro leaves
2 cups shredded romaine lettuce
1 cup (4 ounces) shredded Monterey Jack cheese (optional)

Preheat oven to 400°F. Wrap tortillas in foil, place in oven, and warm while you prepare filling.

In a medium saucepan, heat oil over medium heat. Add green onions and garlic, and cook for 1 minute until fragrant. Stir in beans, chipotle, and 1 cup water. Bring to a simmer, season with salt and pepper, and simmer for 5–7 minutes until slightly thickened and hot. Add salsa (if desired), corn, and lime juice. Cook until heated through.

Unwrap tortillas, and spread yogurt over one side. Top with warm bean mixture, cilantro leaves, lettuce, and cheese (if using). Fold tortillas over and serve 2 per person with additional salsa and chipotle, if desired.

Per serving: 593 calories; 28 g protein; 17 g fat; 82 g carb; 11 g fiber.

Black Rice with Cranberries, Carrots, and Ginger

Fiber is important for a healthy diet. It helps control blood sugar and aids in weight loss. This dish provides 8 grams of fiber per serving. You can find black rice at health food stores or gourmet shops. If you don't have black rice, feel free to substitute with brown rice. You can be creative with other ingredients in this recipe, too. Try adding chopped nuts such as almonds, pecans, or toasted pine nuts. For more color, garnish with chopped parsley.

Serves 4

3 tablespoons olive oil

2 tablespoons finely minced ginger

1 cup diced fresh oyster or shiitake mushrooms

3 medium carrots, cut into ¼-inch cubes

½ cup minced onion

2 celery stalks, cut into ¼-inch cubes

Salt and pepper to taste

3 cups cooked black rice (see grain cooking guide on page 17)

1 cup fresh orange juice

1 cup dried cranberries

¼ cup toasted nuts (optional)

Preheat oven to 325°F.

In a large skillet, heat oil over medium heat, swirling pan to coat. Add ginger and cook until fragrant, about 30 seconds. Add mushrooms and sauté for 1 minute. Add carrots, onion, and celery. Season with salt and pepper. Stir-fry until vegetables are tender, about 5 minutes. Stir in cooked rice, orange juice, and cranberries. Toss to mix well.

Pour rice mixture into a 9x13-inch baking dish. Cover loosely with foil and bake until heated through and liquid evaporates, about 30 minutes. Garnish with nuts, if desired, and serve warm.

Per serving: 441 calories; 8 g protein; 16 g fat; 71 g carb; 8 g fiber.

Wasabi Salmon with Miso-Sesame Sauce

On a recent trip to Japan, a neighborhood restaurant served me pan-fried sardines with miso-sesame sauce, garnished with cherry blossoms. Since it is not always easy to find fresh sardines or cherry blossoms, I made my own version with salmon and colorful flowers from my garden. Wasabi is available in Asian grocery stores and natural food stores.

Serves 4

Miso-Sesame Sauce:
1½ tablespoons red miso paste
¼ cup soy milk
1½ tablespoons toasted sesame seeds

1½ tablespoons minced fresh ginger
1 teaspoon cayenne pepper
¼ cup sake
2 tablespoons tamari
2 tablespoons wasabi paste or powder
4 (4-ounce) salmon fillets
Edible fresh flowers, rinsed, to garnish

In a small bowl, combine miso paste, soy milk, and sesame seeds. Stir until miso is completely dissolved. Set aside.

Combine ginger, cayenne pepper, sake, tamari, and wasabi in a large zippered plastic bag. Blend well. Add salmon, seal bag, and toss to coat. Marinate in refrigerator for 1 hour.

Preheat oven to 400°F. Place salmon on a greased baking sheet, discarding marinade. Bake until fish flakes easily with a fork, about 13 minutes. Remove salmon from oven and transfer to a warm serving plate. Drizzle miso-sesame sauce over fillets. Garnish with flowers. Serve warm with cooked grains of your choice.

Per serving: 246 calories; 34 g protein; 7 g fat; 5 g carb; 1 g fiber.

Desserts in a Flash

Fresh fruit, dark chocolate, and nuts are good choices for a quick and healthy treat. The best part is they require no added sugar and are good for you, so they don't have to be limited to dessert. Sometimes my family and I enjoy them after a workout or even with breakfast. Here is a handful of quick treats that will satisfy a sweet tooth in a healthy way.

Strawberries Dipped in Dark Chocolate

Melt 6 ounces of 60% dark chocolate in a small bowl in the microwave or in a small saucepan over low heat on the stovetop. Dip 1 pound strawberries with stems (about 18 strawberries) in melted chocolate. Set dipped strawberries on a plate and chill in the refrigerator until chocolate sets, about 10 minutes.

Chocolate and Mango with Toasted Almonds

Melt 1½ cups bittersweet chocolate chips in a small bowl in the microwave or in a small saucepan over low heat on the stovetop. Drizzle melted chocolate over 12 ripe mango slices. Garnish with ¼ cup almonds.

Chocolate-Coconut Bananas

Peel and cut 2 ripe bananas into thirds crosswise, pour ½ cup chocolate pudding over top of bananas, and garnish with coconut flakes. Serves 4.

Berries with Soy Ice Cream

Top 2 cups chopped fresh berries with 1 cup soy ice cream. Divide into four serving dishes and garnish with 2 tablespoons toasted sesame seeds or nuts per dish.

Green Tea Ice Cream

Matcha (or maccha) is a Japanese green tea powder traditionally used in tea ceremonies. It is sold at health food stores, Asian grocery stores, and online. If you can't find matcha, you can use the contents of 2 green tea bags. Vigorously mix 2 tablespoons matcha into 2 cups softened vanilla soy or milk ice cream. Return ice cream to freezer for at least 1 hour before serving. Garnish with waffle sticks or ginger cookies (optional).

Blueberries and Yogurt Topped with Pecans

This is my favorite post-workout treat. Some mornings I have it with breakfast. When blueberries are not in season, I use frozen wild blueberries or other frozen fruit such as peaches.

Mix 2 cups fresh blueberries with 1½ cups plain Greek yogurt. Divide into four serving dishes and sprinkle about 1 tablespoon honey-roasted pecans on each dish.

Blueberry Smoothies with Flax Seeds

Place 1 (12.5-ounce) block soft tofu, 1½ cups frozen blueberries, 1 ripe banana, and 1 tablespoon agave nectar or honey in a blender. Blend at high speed until smooth. Pour into 4 glasses and garnish each glass with ½ teaspoon flax seeds. Serve immediately or chill.

TABLE OF EQUIVALENTS

Some of the conversions in these lists have been slightly rounded for measuring convenience.

VOLUME

U.S.	metric
¼ teaspoon	1.25 milliliters
½ teaspoon	2.5 milliliters
¾ teaspoon	3.75 milliliters
1 teaspoon	5 milliliters
1 tablespoon (3 teaspoons)	15 milliliters
2 tablespoons	30 milliliters
3 tablespoons	45 milliliters
1 fluid ounce (2 tablespoons)	30 milliliters
¼ cup (4 tablespoons)	60 milliliters
⅓ cup	80 milliliters
½ cup	120 milliliters
⅔ cup	160 milliliters
1 cup	240 milliliters
2 cups (1 pint)	480 milliliters
4 cups (1 quart or 32 ounces)	960 milliliters
1 gallon (4 quarts)	3.8 liters

WEIGHT:

U.S.	metric
1 ounce (by weight)	28 grams
1 pound	448 grams
2.2 pounds	1 kilogram

LENGTH:

U.S.	metric
⅛ inch	3 millimeters
¼ inch	6 millimeters
½ inch	12 millimeters
1 inch	2.5 centimeters

OVEN TEMPERATURE:

Fahrenheit	Celsius
250	120
275	140
300	150
325	160
350	180
375	190
400	200
425	220
450	230
475	240
500	260

Index

Acknowledgments

Thanks to my talented and hardworking editor, Megan Hiller, who helped build a fire, and added new seasoning to this book. It is truly a great pleasure working with you!

I am very grateful to Mary Baldwin for her magical, resourceful powers in gathering materials, and to Charlotte Cromwell for her gracious help and support.

Vinson, Ming Da, for cooking and sharing many happy meals. Your good appetite fuels my inspiration. Greg, for your continued support and patience.